MONGOOSE

Next Chapter

RAPTURE

BLUEROSE PUBLISHERS
U.K.
Copyright © Fitzroy Wilson 2024

For permissions requests or inquiries regarding this publication, please contact:

BLUEROSE PUBLISHERS
www.BlueRoseONE.com
info@bluerosepublishers.com
+4407342408967

ISBN: 978-93-6452-089-8

Cover design: Daksh
Typesetting: Tanya Raj Upadhyay

First Edition: October 2024

MONGOOSE PROLOGUE

Introduction

For Fitzroy Wilson – Mongoose Rapture-*Next Chapter*

Foreword by Alston A. Hemmings

I truly considered it to be an honor when I first met Fitzroy Wilson in the summer of 1985.

We were both just enrolled as young college students at the Cultural Training Centre- Jamaica School of Drama.

At the time we were studying Theatre Designs, Acting, Caribbean Folk Dance and Voice and Speech among other subjects entailed on the curriculum. The C.T.C would much later evolved into the present day Edna Manley College of the Visual and Performing Arts (E.M.C.V.P.A.). As batch mates, we were drawn to each other, often performing at the "drop of a hat", on campus, concerts, role playing, characters in class drama group, presentations and first year production. Fitzroy's rendition of poems always drew a chorus of applause for his work.

I greatly admired his work then; Now almost forty years later to read his anthology, I can appreciate his words even greater, and the progression of ideas, themes and content displayed in this book. For then, his word sound and rhythm were often based on the non-linear genre of Dub Poetry pattern of the drum score, along with infused baseline of the African conga drum. His style was espoused by fore runners in the vein such as Jean 'Binta' Breese, Claudette Pious, Oku Onoura, Mikey Smith and Muta Baruka/ Linton Kwesi Johnson, et al. I can see that presently his work has undergone significant developmental progress.

The themes explored are everyday concerns of people caught up in the pulse of knowing. The issues are very poignant in your face and cannot be ignored. In his poem *Columbus was no Dub-Master*, The poet, sounds the alarm of the beginning of the European Rapture.

The Fitzroy Wilson-writer, reminds us of how it all started and who's responsible for that adverse,

the initial impact, of white Europeans, on the Caribbean Region.

The harmony and happiness of the native people in their simple way of life was completely extinguished within a 50-year period of Columbus so called discovery of the New World.

When Columbus Deejay

Started to play

It was mayday mayday

All the way

The lyrics was bad

The music was mad

No sweet-sounding pulsating rhythm

Like Arawaks paddling in dug-out canoes

All rocking steady

Ever ready to dance and sing in harmony

Over fish and cassava

In Xamacia

His work speaks volumes in terms of lyrical content, the Caribbean nuances conjured up in an interesting wordplay and double entendres. This body of work shows the human-interest side of the author's concern for humanity.

These poems would resonate with any audience and those in pursuit of Literature and Caribbean History. The offerings are an interesting tapestry in the Spoken Work vein.

The sentiments expressed in the body of work by Fitzroy are a testament of his dedication and determination to publish this second edition of Mongoose Rapture (first published in 2002), but

Mongoose Rapture Next chapter offers so much more.

Jamaica, Guyana and the UK are the three countries, and their historical and political relationships explored that is the feature in this book

Guyana history and is featured the poems Uprising in Demerara, The Walter Rodney uprising is an interesting little remembered story between Jamaica and Guyana, The Oil is Mine reflects the current tension between Guyana and neighbors Venezuela about border dispute

Next Chapter reflects the 21st Century but cut across historical stories, resurrecting real life heroes like Cuffy (Guyana's National Hero) from centuries past with his poem " The Governor of Berbice", At times, The author storytelling of Caribbean history is at its very best.

The Morant Bay uprising showcase Paul Bogle one of Jamaica's National heroes who in 1865 lead the Morant Bay Rebellion to free up education and land for ex slaves in Jamaica.

"I dreamt that my children play alone

In a forest of hungry lions

Where deluded teachers go hunting"

In *Rapture the next Chapter* The poet speaks about the high rate of racists school exclusion policy for Caribbean children in England, It links Paul Bogle fight for the same thing in 1865 in Jamaica. In *Reluctant Mother* the master storyteller tells the Windrush story for the new Arrivals from the Caribbean to England and the way they were treated. He goes much further in the *Windrush Revolution*...reminding the British that it was they who came calling. Much more poignant personal reminder in "***My Daddy was a war hero***" in memory of his father Joel Wilson who fought in the second world war for the British. This is personal, no offence.

Fitzroy, you have done it again.!

I highly recommend this collection of poems as performance pieces to be recited by Primary School children, Youth Speech festivals in speaking ensembles, College and University level students and the adult layman/woman who have an interest in poetry composition and performance.

Readers will find interest in your work and inspiration from the mastery of your craft. I think it is timely for this modern contemporary era and timeless for mass appeal towards futuristic citizens wherever, a pulse beats.

Looking forward to more offerings from the quilt of your pen.

Alston Hemmings
Educator In English Literature and Theatre Arts
Charlemont High School Jamaica
Actor/ Poet/ Stage Manager
Graduate of The Enda Manley School of Performing and Visual Arts

TABLE OF CONTENTS

MONGOOSE

And before the day

When this strange ship anchors in our bay

She

Only seventeen

Sweet and young

Was the queen of our dreams

Until she became the victim of a twisted

tongue

He was going to be our everything

Our Marcus Garvey

Our Martin Luther King

Our next Malcolm X

Until he became barmy

And turn the gun on his own army

For like Judas he could not wait

So

Like a hungry fish he swallows the silver bait

And

Now

Crack

Smack

Our neighbourhood down the middle

Like

A giant hammer and chisel

Now he haunts my children like a giant
shadow

As

If there is no tomorrow

He haunts me

Like a daring duppy in a bamboo tree

Like a fallen angel that broke loose

Like a mongoose

But everybody knows

Everybody knows that mongoose isn't free

Mongoose is just another Jack Horner on my
street corner

Drug dealing and peddling

Mongoose on the loose is a stoolpigeon to a
drive-by shooting

Mongoose is another would-be hero
Turn Zero

RAPTURE NEXT CHAPTER

I dreamt that my children play alone

In a forest of hungry lions

Where deluded teachers go hunting

Smartly dressed in a coat of mis-educated
blood

And the jungle echoes conspire to kill a
dream

But who will decide the colour of my
children dreams

Who will decide which hope to rest in the
cold cemetery of exclusion

Brothers rally round the black, red green and
gold

Let's tell our children the stories that has
never been told

And let not history repeat yet another beat

Let not history repeat a ferry of stolen dream
on a hopeless horizon

Like frozen hope sold on yesterday's auction
block

I woke up

My sweat was cold

My mind boil in a painful turmoil

As I fear that my dreams were real

The spectacle sculpts in modern times

I swear

I swear I will never sleep again

I must exclude the luxury of sleep

It is now very clear to me the way it is going
to be

See

I won't let my children die while I sleep

Sisters rally round the black red green and
gold

Let's tell our children the stories that never
been told

And let not history repeat yet another beat

Let not history repeat a ferry of stolen
dreams on a hopeless horizon

Like frozen hope sold on yesterday's auction
block

Let tell our children about the rapture

Let tell our children how the European
rapture came

The Rapture that captures our great
civilization from our mother

Lets tell our children about the story that has
never been told

COLUMBUS WAS NO DUB-MASTER

When Columbus DeeJay
Started to play
It was mayday mayday
All the way

The lyrics was bad
The music was mad
No sweet sounding pulsating rhythm
Like Arawaks paddling in dug-out canoes
All rocking steady
Ever ready to dance and sing in harmony
Over fish and cassava
In Xamacia

No my friend
Christopher Columbus sound system
Had a wicked and dreadful rhythm
The treble was torture
The base was like a poisonous barracuda
A melody of mass murder
A gripping saga of genocide
Far and wide

From Jamaica to Cuba

Cuba to Hispaniola

The Spanish selector was the Arawaks
exterminator

Columbus was no Dub master

No dub master

But he was a master blaster that blast a great
civilization into oblivion

So

Before

You

Know

The dancehall was empty

Not

One

Arawak Indian in sight

MY DEFINING MOMENT

(For the original people of the Caribbean)

I was there

Long before the melting pot got hot

I went about my business stark naked

In the general scheme of things

This was no big thing

It was the norm

It was natural as a sour green mango turn
ripe and sweet

As the days before Eve seduce Adam in a
grass mini skirt

Before he ate her apple

Before Colombus came as serpent looking
for Gold

Before Europe came as cold sex starved
rapist

Before they came as murders

This Caribbean was Eden

Then they destroy the garden to build the
garrison

I am now a silent symphony

A haunted legacy like teardrops turn rain

Rain came

Turn holocaust hurricane

Synonymous with fallen trees

I am like a lost dream that floats
downstream

Fading fast as cultures converge

New identities emerge

They build their houses on the grave of the
brave

Sleepless spirit now rants with rage

Haunts in restless dark clouds

Mystic complains with wind and rain

UPRISING IN DEMERARA

(For Quamina Gladstone Born Ghana 1778)

I saw an uprising in Demerara

For

Black people wanted to be free

In Eighteen twenty-three

Today

In their Market Places

I saw the fear in their white faces

As

They kill Quamina

The Carpenter in Demerara

Yesterday

The hurricane came

Inhumane

Yesterday

The hurricane came

Insane

To feed the hungry mouth of King sugarcane

Yesterday was when I saw the wild wicked
wind

Swept the West African plain

I saw a boy Quamina and his mother in
chain

Captured by the wild wicked wind

Quamina in pain deep in the belly of King
Sugarcane

No joy for this little boy

With a shackle around his neck

Quamina

Trapped in the dark dungeon of shame

Say

I remember the day

When the hurricane came across the middle
passage

To blow away my tomorrow

When the wicked wind spat sad sorrow in
Quamina little face

When the Hurricane blow Quamina

Quamina the little lad without his dad

The Hurricane Blow Quamina from Ghana

All the way across the Atlantic to Guyana

To feed

The need

Of big

Sugar Slavery in Demerara

Today

I saw them killing Quamina the man from
Guyana

I saw how they fear Quamina in Demerara

In a September to remember

THE GOVERNOR OF BERBICE

Cuffy's fate
Was to die in the same year he became great
The year of our lord Seventeen Sixty-Three

Cuffy is symbolic
Cause
Cuffy Uprising was the Caribbean First thirst
Cause
Cuffy iconic uprising was the symbolic tonic
I drank to free me

Cuffy erupt like a volcano to start the tempo
When the first blow for freedom strike

Twenty-eight years later
Toussant L Overture pick up the tempo
To
become the Caribbean first black supremo

On that day as I watch the relay
I saw
I am sure
Cuffy pass the baton to Toussant L overture
I swore I saw Cuffy implore
Toussant L overture to do much more

If I was to be free

From the treachery of slavery

Cuffy was

The uncompromising leader of my uprising

Cuffy was too much for the Dutch

It was so surprising

When Cuffy unsmiling

Without notice

Declare himself Governor of Berbice

YOUR WAR HAS NO HEROES

Europe came as Warmonger
Who had the hunger
Five hundred years of hungry desire to be
the devil

You war evil on Paul bogle
You war evil on George William Gordon in
Morant Bay
Multiplying the wisdom of evil with an open
bible
But hear me when I say today
Your war had no heroes

You will find you only make martyrs of me
See
The fruits of your labor
Was the murder of another in Montego Bay
Yet
Another Lynching after an Uprising
You murder Sam Sharpe my big brother
You erase a native race
To enslave another
Your aim
To maim
To kill at will

To have a bloody bellyful
Until

Today
Still you bring back body bags
Your own children lost forever like logs on a
slipstream
Deliberate deliverer of evil
If you clip the wings of the eagle
The eagle of your egos
You will find your war has no heroes

When you try to erase Martin Luther King
Here is the Thing
When Bob Marley Sing
Nanny of the Maroons still stand tall
We still hear Marcus Garvey Call
While we watch your Apartheid fall

When you see
Me coming like a runaway train and you will
feel the strain
You will still
Feel the indomitable spirit of Nelson
Mandela
Even when
You killed Steve Biko
You will find you only make martyrs of me
Your war has no heroes

Europe

You came as Warmonger

Who had the hunger to enslave an African
Warrior

You took many trips

You carry me like tin sausage on your sailing
cargo ships

You carry me across the middle passage like
the spoils of war

Your illegal raid to create your empire

From an Atlantic slave trade

While I create an angry silent revolution in
me

A burning desire like fire to roam free like a
lion once more

To Kick off your front door

To suffer poor no more

I renounce your persecution

I am advocating my own solution

To burn your big great white house

Just before you put two spoons of sugar in
your tea

The same King Sugarcane that enslaves me

I shall burn your big white house on the top
of your evil hill

Until

Europe came as Warmonger

Who had the hunger

Five hundred years of hungry desire to be
the devil

I shall redeem the Indomitable spirits of
Kings

Trapped inside

The royalty of my pride

A pride that

Rides me like an explosion

My dignity

Bursting for a revolution

If

You unsettle your little metal steaming kettle

Your little tea kettle will dream a revolution

Listen to I when I say today

I and I

Royal Rasta man steams a righteous
revolution

Just like your holy bible

First you trouble I the Lion while I and I
sleep

Just know I will rebel and trouble you when
I and I leap

So don't be surprised when I mumble a
bubble that you first ignore

More and more I won't even wait until you
snore

I am your boiling unsettle kettle like roots
reggae

Here I when I say today the sound system
sounds sweet in revolution street
This freedom medley is cool and deadly in
the dance
When every man has a chance to vote
This musical note to his own narrative
I play today my own agenda

This freedom mystic music is making my
bubble reaching boiling point
Sorry to disappoint
I anoint a revolution audacious like Cuffy
I rumble a revolution like Marcus Mosiah
Garvey
But still
You won't hear my silent footsteps even
when I am near
You won't hear me coming up the hill
Until
I rumble a revolution from your own
concrete Jungle

Europe came as Warmonger
Who had the hunger
Five hundred years of hungry desire to be
the devil

Now I can't stop you urinating evil on I
Pissing like rancid rain way up from your sky

You are too blind to see
Me
This little speck of humanity
Too blind to see
Me
Too arrogant to understand your own
insanity
So instead
You count the dead
Body bags of your own children
Lost forever like logs in a slipstream

Your war has no heroes
Only confusion like a red river in your head
A red delusion of Grandeur
Depend on the political side you ride
Of the deep divide
Of this terrible tide
Don't be too blind to see
The defenseless child inside of me
Screaming in the land of the burning flesh
The beautiful little child
Who wants to live
To give to a better world

THE OIL IS MINE

This little oil of mine
I am going to let it shine
This oil finds of mine
I am going to let it shine

They find oil in a Guyana
But
Blood a boil in a Venezuela
Venezuela proclaims
Like a weird video game
That
The oil is mine

Venezuela proclaims
I own that land a long time
So
This oil is mine
All mine

Venezuela proclaims
I was only playing the waiting game
Such a shame
For
The oil is mine
All mine
For I own this land a long time

Venezuela proclaims
Venezuela claim
That
Two thirds of Guyana
Should be at least be in Venezuela maiden
name
For the oil is mine
All mine

Venezuela proclaims
For when there was the partition
Follow by the separation
No one endorse the divorce decree
See
Now you will agree
That the oil is for Venezuela guarantee

Venezuela proclaims
Venezuela claim
Like a weird video game
The oil is mine
All mine

Guyana says
I disagree

This little oil of mine
I am going to let it shine

Don't come with your trickery
Your skulduggery
And you foolish old story
That almost all of our country
Now become Venezuelan Territory

Understand Spanish Man
That this is English Guyana land
Not Venezuelan

Are you a fool
That didn't go to school
Check the International rule
You can't claim land
As Venezuelan
If for over a hundred years the world agrees
That Guyana is the rightful trustee

This land can never be Venezuelan
when it is such a crucial part of Guyana's
identity
So
This little oil of mine
I am going to let it shine
This oil finds of mine
I am going to let it shine

THE FALLEN APPLE

Yesterday
Satan saw Eve walking in my front garden
Walking stark naked
And lust was a candle that became a flame
Flame became a furious fire of forbidden
desire
And my world was never the same

When the apple is ripe it will fall from the
tree
But if you shake
Tease
Or if you climb to the treetop
The apple will drop before the time

She shakes
Her ecstasy grips like an earthquake
As she discovers pleasure is the treasure
below the waist

Now Satan is asleep
She shivers
And for the first time
Eve
was
cold

HUMPTY DUMPTY I AM NOT

Poverty is a prison
You shut me in
You shut me out like heaven keeping out sin

You always have the upper hand
Land
Is your powerful right hand

If I own no land
You hook me with an upper cut
Just before your headbutt
You viciously attack me with my handcuffed
hand behind my back

Poverty is a sin
Your poison pin like heroin nasty needle
Your tax is my poison
My poverty indictment prison
A rope around my neck like a bounce cheque

My life sentence is from your government
A life sentence of deep solitary confinement
You and your clique
Drugged me up like a zombie duppy

Try to keep me asleep behind your bleak
prison wall

But

I am a freak with a strong physique

I will never sleep like a weak blind sheep

I am unique so I have a strong desire to leap

Leap higher like a raging fire to peep

Soaring like a flying bird over your steep tall
wall

Every time I try to climb higher

You pull away the ladder

Like

A clumsy humpty dumpty

Down

I fall into your miserable mire

But

Humpty Dumpty I am not

A strong desire I have got

I am a hot freak with a strong physique

I am so unique

My desire is on fire to leap

This is no great fall off your tall wall

Bare feet I walk

On a bumpy dumpty road
But
Humpty Dumpty I am not
A strong desire I have got

As it goes
I just buck my toes
It won't be long
That I get myself together again
It is not time for my story to end

I am not daydreaming about your glass
ceiling
No more feeling
About life's lucky healing

So sorry
I am not waiting no more
To win your lottery

Cause I am unique with a strong physique
When I fall
I fall on my feet

I am a sweet little bird
So complete
Like an elite athlete
I have got wings

So
Your tall wall
Like London Bridge is burning down

My desire is on fire
So
I fly high
Soaring in the sky
So
High
Way up above your
Lie

ATTACK ME AT YOUR OWN RISK

When you bite my skin like ticks

Attacker

Attack me at your own risk

For I have got your address

And you going to get stress

So

When you mess with me and put me to the
test

Be prepare to mess with your best

For be aware that I am bless

Yes

I have blessing from the best

You cough up evil like the spirit of the devil

But a rule of evil will never be forever

And

I am not going to be no bodies victim

You hear

You hear

When you knock me down

I will never stay down

For if I am not on the ground

You can't trample

And

Make of me an example

If I am not on the ground

You can't crush my pride

By extinguishing my fire inside

Like malaria mosquitoes sucking for a
bloody bellyful

You are here to buck me

Like a big bad bull

You want to minus me by multiplying my
misery

You can't allow me by leaving me be

You must a fancy me

Like how you fancy a cup a tea

But sooner or later if you fancy too much tea
you going to wee-wee

But a tell you

you nah wee-wee on me

Sooner or later

you going to have a belly ache from the evil
Tea- cake you always bake

And I sincerely hope when you poo

You will find no tissue is in the loo

ZINC FENCE

I don't want to seem unwittingly unkind
In other people's mind
About my life in transition
The transition of my ambition is like a
Guyanese oil find
About
The turning of my tide
The turning point of my pride
Yet Another
Adjustments in my mindset
From
A shitty Zinc fence mentality
To a white picket fence in just one sentence

I can't lie
I have to tell you
I tried to paint my old Zinc fence white
But somehow it still didn't feel right
So
I had to face it
I had to replace it
I had to replace my long-forgotten history
My Granny legacy
With a beautiful brand new me

Just like Granny cassava bammy
Some Cassava look deceptively delicious
But can be so poisonous

Some Cassava is like a barracuda
A bit like if you choose to use brute force
To open
To free
Jamaican Ackee
From off the Jamaican Ackee tree

But stick a pin
Before you think everything is dim
Not my Granny Bammy

My Granny bammy was yummy
My Granny Bammy was so yummy
Yummy in my little tummy
Yet
I love it no more in my big belly
I love no more my Granny Bammy in my big
belly

Instead
I now love nice Guyanese brown rice Cook-
up
I love Barbados dark Rum
I love it in my big belly

Like Guyanese Golden Apple turn Jamaican
June plum

My big belly
Don't like eating Corolla in Guyana
But my big belly
Love drinking Cerace Tea in Jamaica

Same difference
Different lingo
Different name but same mango
Like Pigeon peas is the same as Gungo

I replaced many years of my dead departed
Granny old Zinc fence in my yard
And
In truth
it wasn't that hard
It was just like using a debit card
When you have money in the bank
Water in the tank like a bank overdraft

It was without a guilty plea in me
See
I now acknowledge the brand new me
without apology
Like buying something new from the store
Like Exon finding more oil in a Guyanese
river

You get more than just another receipt
Because
You deserve something nice
When you have paid the right price
So
I have change over the years
Without a tear
Without a fear
From the inside out without a shout
Leaving my old Zinc fence behind

In the end my friend
This could be contrived by many a mind
To be unwittingly unkind
To the history of my own legacy
But
I have change over the years
Without any tears
Without any fears
From the inside out without a doubt about
leaving my old Zinc fence behind

Upgraded pride
Upgraded ride outside
Brand-new air-conditioned mind inside
Yes
I have changed

And so have you also
Even though you now pretend
My good old friend

In the end
My good old friend
I don't want to seem unknowingly unkind
But I hope you realise
That
I am not going to apologise
Not
Feeling guilty about the turning of my tide
Never
Ever Judge me about the turning of my
upgraded pride
Judge me not about the changes in my
mindset
From shitty Zinc fence mentality
To a white picket fence in one sentence

GEORGETOWN GUYANA

I visit Georgetown

Not as a Tourist

Georgetown was just on my list

I cannot lie

Visiting Guyana

The English-speaking Caribbean in South
America

Was one of the hundred things

I needed to do before I die

I wanted to see Georgetown in Guyana

As a little boy in Jamaica

I remember Bourda

Mostly rain no play but a wicket with a lot of
runs for the batsmen

Batsmen like Sarwan and Alvin Kallicharan

I wanted to visit Georgetown

I wanted to see the city of the great Rohan
Khani

I visit Georgetown

Saw Forbes Burham Father of the Nation

I saw his final resting place

I saw the city of the great Cheddi Jagan the
Indian
City of many faces

I saw big billboards of one united Guyana
Georgetown not Berbice now is the great
Cuffy hometown
Cuffy statue stand tall in Georgetown

I visit Georgetown
Now a sprawling city
Once the English Darling of South America
Georgetown was built by the blood of Africa
Georgetown was built by the sweat of India
I visit Georgetown where so many others are
now my Caricom Brothers
So
Before I could even sneeze
There were hosts of marching Portuguese
Who are also Guyanese

THE POET MASTURBATE

The poet hears voices
Voices without words like birds without
wings
The poet embraces words
For he is lonely
The poet has no playmate to embrace
So
He plays with words
Masturbating literary
To literary masturbate
It is like having an intense conversation
With oneself in the dark
To the sound of distant applause

When the poet is lonely
He embrace's himself
Like new lovers entwined in body and mind

For the poet is a lover of words
Words
That he will verbally ejaculate
Words
That are dreams of passion

And

When his dreams are no more in black and
white

But

Are in live and living colour

They become virtual visions of silent
seduction

Then

The poets masturbate

And

Poetry climax

A gushing innermost crescendo caught on
CCTV

My dreams are no more in black and white

I dream in live and living colour

I dream that a dreary day will turn into a
wonderful night

Yet I see

In my dreams a crowd of lonely people in a
world full of people

So many unhappy people in happy families

So many smiling faces with unsmiling hearts

CHURCHILL CONSPIRACY

(For Cheddi Jagan)

I spy
I spy with my left eye
The little irony
The day Winston Churchill anxiety
Try to kill democracy in British Guiana

History proclaims with great acclaim
The hypocrisy of Western foreign policy
Spinning
The lies and more lies
The false prophecy of spies

The western autocracy
Told us
That they had replaced
Their disgrace plantocracy
With our great democracy

Now let's shine the light
Switch on the spotlight
Let the dark night of our history burn bright
Let burn bright like Guyana sunlight

Just open our history door once more
Just let us explore this question
Once more just to be sure

Was Cheddi Jagan really an agent of
communist conspiracy?

To spread communism in Churchill British
Colony
Or
Was it Winston Churchill brilliant bigotry
That needed
To
Chop with a machete Cheddi Jagan audacity

To shine the light on British Guiana workers'
plight
To stop Jagan fight
For Guyana Workers right

I spy
I spy
With my left eye
The big little lie

When
History proclaimed this irony
That
The same beacon of democracy

The same Communist haters hypocrisy
This hypocrisy of Western foreign policy
The hypocrisy of their anxiety
The fear about communist conspiracy

Western foreign policy
Communist haters
Went on to create deadly dictators

Dictators In Nicaragua
History proclaims the same
Shame
In Argentina
History proclaims the same
Shame
In
Venezuela
The conspiracy of fear
Just like Churchill anxiety

Isn't Democracy a mockery
If you replace it With MAGA Autocracy?
Isn't Democracy a mockery If you replace it
with Trumpism racist policy?

Democracy was a mockery with Winston
Churchill Conspiracy

JAMAICAN JOSHUA

(for Michael Manley)

Joshua row the boat ashore Alleluia
Joshua row the boat ashore Alleluia
The hurricane came
The hurricane came Joshua was his name

Hail the man
Who came to slay the dragon of imperialism
Armed with socialism in his bush-jacket

Joshua was the preaching politician
On the reggae musical bandwagon
Who came to slay the dragon

Joshua came with his rod of correction
Joshua came with political seduction
Joshua came with a simple solution
For
Better must come not only for some

But
More power for the poor
More power for the people that are poor
But

The people with the power
Just empty their ivory tower
Every hour
And
leave Jamaican poor people without even
flour

Money migrates
To the great United State
At an astonishing rate
Leaving JA
To face a deadly fate

Long before Joshua could-a close the gate
Long before Joshua could-a close the gate

Then
The oil
Jamica rely on to survive or die
Fly sky high
that not even the rich country could a buy

In came in the IMF
With their sternest test
Plunging Jamaica into mess after mess

Until the day Joshua tried to break away

Joshua row the boat ashore.. alleluia
Joshua row the boat ashore... alleluia

But every time Joshua row the boat ashore
The loan shark took away the oar
And bore a bigger hole

The boat start leaks
And when Pickney hungry
Pickney weak
Pickney can't even play hide and seek
When Pickney can't get food to eat

Sunday dinner became chicken –back and
rice an peas
Joshua the situation tried to ease
He started land lease to give poor people
land to farm food
But by now Joshua Please
Even the coconut trees were dying of disease

Joshua got friendly with Cuba
Comrade Castro gave Jamaica some milk
called La Crema
And just like Hay fever
That really got up the nose hole of America

While America and the CIA
Was a wail them tail

An a jump an rail

Joshua full of charisma wail "we are not for sale"

Amidst media communism propaganda

Joshua took Jamaica bauxite to Russia

In exchange for some cars call Lada

Joshua fight day and night

For what he thought was right

To bridge the gap between the bottom and top

MORANT BAY UPRISING

Back in eighteen sixty-five
Paul Bogle was the leader of my tribe
He tried to meet with the English governor
Eyrie
So
All the brother and sister could get some
food to eat
He and many other men then walk bare feet

Through the gully
Through the bush
Through the sun
Through rain he walked in vain
From Stony Gut to Spanish Town
And then back to Morant Bay he came again
And burn the courthouse down
And burn the courthouse down

For like me Bogle could a see
That though they say that we are free from
slavery
There will always be some strange
conspiracy
That enslave me

Black people were free since eighteen thirty
eight

But England still close the school gate

No health

No wealth

No land for a black man

Today

It is the same conspiracy that cause the
tribal war in a Kingston

It is the same conspiracy that cause the
uprising in a Brixton

Today I see the same conspiracy

Conspiracy in their smiling faces

As they drugged me up in their mental
institution

Conspiracy as they try to lock me up in their
prison

And I see a conspiracy coming straight at me
even from my TV

When the British Government create their
hostile environment

To rob me of my equal rights

So

They hang Bogle in Eighteen Sixty-five

They call me an undocumented immigrant in
nineteen ninety-five

So I see the same conspiracy

If you have the audacity to fight for your
human right

You are mad

You are bad

For when a black man dreams of freedom

He is an arrogant deviant

I still dream the same abnormal dream as
Paul Bogle

We dance the same abnormal rude boy
dance

A race fighting for a place at the top table

EMPTY BASKET CAN'T CARRY WATER

On that sad August day
White Christianity had a chance
To treat glad Black Humanity with human dignity
But White Christianity
Deliberately missed that opportunity

White Christianity
Instead
As history shown
Just double down
To treat black freedom with impunity
See
Freedom was murdered
Just like another lynching
The murderer walks free saying Amen
Free like white church choir singing
Amazing grace self- forgiving hymn in dim moonlight
The Slave masters
Was not even charge with manslaughter
When Freedom comes up empty
Like black people drinking kool-aid turn salt seawater

For
Black man basket was empty
I still hear the English Laughter
Send the fool a little further
He is not wise to realize
That
Empty basket can't carry water
Black man basket was empty
Black freedom hope
Was like a rope that choke a plenty
For Blackman had the audacity
To be wanting to be free
From the brutality of European slavery

So long
In the Caribbean human slavery was
England's prosperity
Now Black people had the audacity to stop
being England's property

No one really care about counting the cost
Even now
of
400 years of our black human holocaust

Meanwhile
While Blackman basket was empty
Slave Master basket as usual
Was full a plenty

For Black freedom was a shocking mockery
The British Government was so happy to compensate
Financially
Slave master for the loss of their human property

Actually
They financially Compensate
Four hundred years of brutality and hate
They
Compensate white western Christianity
For the loss of slavery

It's never ever too late for European
To compensate the Caribbean
For four hundred years of state sponsored hate
It's never ever too late
To
Financially compensate
Slaves
Descendant loss of human liberty
For
Black man basket still empty
I can still hear the English laughter
Empty basket can't carry water

THE RELUCTANT MOTHER

(For the Windrush Generation)

Take a trip
Take a trip Caribbean man
Please come to England as fast as you can

We have jobs for the woman
We have jobs for the man
So please get to England as fast as you can

He took a trip
He took a trip on the cargo ship
Caribbean man got to England as fast as he
could
As his English mother said he should
But
When he got there
The
Promised land was a nightmare
He
Went to rent a room
But
Found it easier to jump over the moon
It was a bit strange
For

Down at the labour exchange
He
Always got the job with the low pay
Nevertheless
He worked very hard to pave the way
To
Send for his lover to come over
But
The future was bleak
For
She had to work six days a week
Ten hours a day for even a lower pay
As
Well as working at home all alone
And
When the children came
Neighbours start to complain
Racism
Became a hurricane
The hurricane jumped and prance
And kick up a fuss
And
When snow didn't fall for Christmas
Caribbean man got the blame

Take a trip
Take a trip Caribbean man

You better leave England
As fast as you can

Fly away
Go away
Don't you ever come back another day

For powerful Powell has come out to play
With his visions of rivers of blood
Flowing on the banks of the inner city

But
Caribbean man
Caribbean woman rose like a lion
Harder than iron
Standing tall
Fighting with their backs against the wall
Giving voice to the oppressed
The dispossessed
Changing the shape of the landscape of the
reluctant mother
For ever and ever... Amen

THE WINDRUSH REVOLUTION

We didn't come from over the ocean

We didn't come from over the sea

We didn't come here just to drink your
English Tea

You say one thing

Then you fling another like people in Guyana

Eating Iguiana

And telling me from Jamaica that they don't
eat Lizard

We are the same black people who came in
England's name

We are the same people who came when yuh
calling

We are the same people who came when yuh
bawling

We are the same people who came when you
limping

When Hitler nearly bruk yuh foot

So put that under yuh little hat on yuh big
English head

Lest yuh forget that

Put that under your little hat but never
forget that

When yuh start chat

When you ramp up our overflowing cup
When you turn up
Turn up the volume so others can only
assume
When you rant and rave that I am only an
immigrant
That just come to rob a poor white of his job

Ramping up the rhetoric with your own
narrative
They believe your story
for they know not their own history
That we are the same people who came in
England's name
To work in your factory

Don't forget a who yuh talking to
When
You ramp up your rhetoric's
With your racial politics

With a twisted mouth you shout at me
Like a loudmouth farmer on the hill
In an insane drought
Praying for a pill that will ease the pain
But complaining about too much rain
flooding the plain

We are the same people who came
When you came calling like Prince Charming
We are the same people who came when you
were bawling

We are the same people who came when you
were limping
When Hitler nearly bruk yuh foot

We came like the Windrush
To work on your railway
We came like the Windrush
To heal your motorway

We didn't just appear from nowhere
We hear you calling
You
Shouting loud
We were so proud to stop you from falling
Yuh say come here
So
We come from far
We come from near when yuh seh come here

We come from far like the rain to stop your
star
From falling
We came when we hear you calling
We came because you were bawling

We answer your plea

You were on bending knee

We didn't come from across the Ocean

Over the sea

Just to drink your English tea

Yuh call we when yuh was a beg we

Yuh tell we yuh a we commonwealth family

Yuh tell we that commonwealth community
was a single entity

Yuh tell we that you repent

So we forgive you

Yuh seh slavery was a disgrace

And now yuh didn't mind our black face

Work is a plenty

Let us work in unity

As one aim

One destiny

Now

It's a shame that you forget we came in your
name

Such a shame

That you forget without regret

That we are the same people you colonise
and despise

Once again

My English Friend

You come to reject your Subject
And once again
Your government choose
To abuse and refuse me of my entitlement
You
Come to dump me like garbage
Turning
Up your nose like you smell rotten cabbage
So
Remember that
Put it under your little hat
Memba dat
It was you who slave me
Just to put some suga in yuh English tea
Memba Dat big Shot
We were the solution
To finance your industrial Revolution

Memba Dat before yuh start to chat
Memba Dat
When you start to ramp up your rhetoric
Memba Dat
When you ramp up your sick racist politics
Every time you call
Every time you bawl
We are the people who came from afar more
and more to restore
We are the people who saw your pain

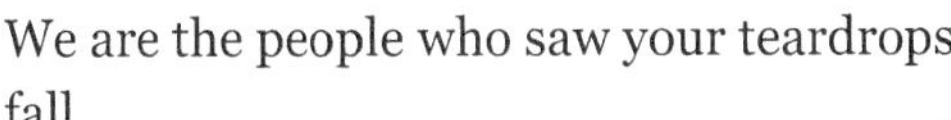

We are the people who saw your teardrops
fall

Fall like Portland rain

Yes

We only came in England's name

MY PAPA WAS A WAR HERO

(for Joel Wilson)

My papa had fire in his belly

So

When papa hear England a holler over the
ocean

Papa like many other ran to help 'him
mother

England was a shout

A shout

A shout

Deep down from the shadow of Hitler's
mouth

This was the time when England' require the
service of black men from her empire

My papa had fire in his belly

Papa like many other

Had this strange desire

To die for king and country

My papa travelled far

To fight a world war

An when the war was won

England's' hang a wreath of medals upon his
breast

He returned home a local hero
Telling tales of war and adventure afar
Papa fought proud in England's name
He had changed someone's world
But his own world remained the same

CRICKET KINGS

Cricket sweet
When West Indies a dweet
Blow by blow
Clive Llyod let them know
Who is the champion

Michael Holding when him was bowling
Made batsmen fret because he was
whispering death

Bouncers flying
Batmen walking

Ask England about the back-to-back
blackwash
Even Australia get lash

Malcolm Marshall him didn't partial
Big bird Garner had the wickedest Yorker
An Colin Croft wasn't soft

And
When Winston Davis was in the side
He bowled with ferocious pride
King Viv Richard was smoking Joe the boss

Lawrence Rowe was a touch of class

And

There was a little Indian man called Alvin
Kallicharan

For twenty years

West Indies was the best in the test

Was far better than all the rest

These guys were the cream

They were more than a cricket team

A perfect cricket dream

Roy Fredricks master of the hook

Yet him didn't did it by the book

Gordon Greenidge and Desmond Haynes
most awesome openers

Jeffery Dujon one of the great wicket keepers

While all others were blazing bulldozers

By contrast Larry Gomes

Was the quiet nice little sheet anchor

That made the team stubbornly stronger

Gus Logie was great fielder

When West Indies was cricket leader

No nation had a hope

No nation could a cope

So

ICC decide to change the cricket rules

So

That others can catch up

So

Barking snarling bouncers became timid
little pup

Lords empty the bullets from the gun

Lords snatch away the fun

So

Batsmen who use to run away

All the way to square leg

Batsmen who use to cringe and beg

Batsmen with terrible technique

Suddenly became unique

Boy

Many batsmen start to jump for joy

Helmet get bigger and filledwith grill

Bat gets wider

You got side pad

Chest pad

Thigh pad

This pad

That pad

Yet only one bouncer per over

WINDOW SHOPPING

Year after Year
As I walk on the shoulders of my ancestors

I have waited outside your shop window
To look in on your latest fashion
Stepping outside my own definition of
myself
To see
What others have cleverly made of me
Yet
I dream that my mind mirrors are far better
Far better of reflecting me than shop
windows
Shop windows generally speculate
A reflection interprets only one solitary
image
And bingo the meaning of my whole story
This I dream can be contrived
Just like a mannequin existence

I feel shop windows cannot taste
Cannot really taste all the contradictions of
my ingredients
Cannot see the sunrise of my wandering
heart

Cannot really see my hidden hills of solitude

Cannot walk with me in the valley of my
experience

Cannot tell very well what mask I wear today

So do I try to shoplift your version of me

To look for myself in the faces of strangers

Yesterday

It strikes me like a lightning Usain Bolt

Today it feels

Like a perfect square drive from Brian Lara

That

Perhaps in search of my perfect self

I silently daydream not to walk alone

So today

As I walk on the shoulders of my Ancestors

On this great journey of myself discovery

Contradictions will rise like mountains with
wings

Torture like an eagle caged in my heart

And though I may often look in at your shop
window

I will always return to the windows of my
mind

PEOPLE TALKING IN MY HEAD

Roll River Jordon roll
Roll River Jordon roll
Roll River Jordon roll
Roll River Jordon roll

Fall rain fall
Wet-up me worries when it a get too tall
Seh to
Wet-up me worries it a get too tall
Seh to cool de steam
Seh to Cool the steam
of this wicked dream
Healing stream
Hear my scream

Wash away de pain
De shackles and de chain
De Stress an de strain from me brain
De Stress and de strain from me brain

For my mind is sinking in a painful turmoil
Naked fear is twisting my brain with pain

For a got people talking in my head
Spiteful Strangers on a mission
Having conversation without my permission

People talking in my head
And now
I rather be dead

People talking in my head
People talking in my head
People talking in my head
People talking in my head

Dem a trample pon me brain
Jus a trample pon me brain
A trample pon me brain an me feel insane

People talking in my head
People talking in my head
People talking in my head
People talking in my head

Roll River Jordon Roll
Roll River Jordon Roll
Roll River Jordon Roll
Roll River Jordon Roll

Fall rain fall
Se to wet-up me worries

It a get too tall
Se to wet-up me worries it a get too tall

Se to cool de steam
Se to cool de steam
Of this wicked dream

Healing stream
Hear my scream
Wash away de pain
The shackles an de chain
De stress an de strain from me brain
De stress an de strain from me brain

For naked fear is twisting my brain with pain

For I got squatters squatting in my brain
Squatters squatting in my brain

Say
I want to complain
For I got squatters squatting in my brain

Squatters Squatting
Preachers preaching
Women walking
Dogs are barking
Lions chasing
Terror stalking
voices calling
People parking
Without displaying
They parking for free

To persecute me
And nobody feels but me
Nobody hears but me
Nobody feels but me
Nobody hears but me

People talking in my head
People talking in my head
People talking in my head
People talking in my head

Dem a trample pon me brain
Jus a trample pon me brain
A trample pon me brain and a feel insane

People talking in my head
People talking in my head
People talking in my head
People talking in my head

This is a strange episode
Of a heavy load on a rocky road

An
A want to fly away
fly away
fly away
fly away from myself

Fly away
Fly away
Fly away
Fly away from myself

LAST ORDERS

Ano go me a go

A come me a come

Ano go me a go

A come me a come

Even if me shoes a beg bread

An a got a tumor in my head

I still prefer to be to be alive than dead

Ano go me a go

A come me a come

Ano go me ago

A come me a come

So me nah go commit no suicide

Me jusa go sidung a wait for the turning tide

Me nah tek nuh early ride into nuh sunset

Cause fe mi time no come yet

Not till God tell me that me blow me last
breath

Ano go me a go

A come me a come

Ano go me a go

A come me a come

Although sometime me get scared and a fret

Because me can't get rid of the bad breath

An me Missis sometime seh me nuh have
nothing more a get

Me nah go tun nuh duppy rolling calf

An mek god laugh

Ano go me a go

A come me a come

Ano go me a go

A come me a come

Even if A got a tumor in my head

An prefer to be alive than dead

Me nah leave yah before me time

Not before my bell start chime

I prefer to suck the lemon

To suck the lime until the right time

Until the right time

Ano go me a go

A come me a come

Ano go me a go

A come me a come

RASTA CELEBRATION

Rasta rise to the occasion

With a nyabinghi celebration

Minds a meet

Drums a beat

Music sweet

At Selassie I feet

Rasta rose from the shacks

Fight off the ignorant attacks

For the man in the knitted-tam is no
blackheart man

I and I is a still small voice from the shanty

With peace an love a plenty

Alienated by rejection in the slums of
urbanization

Even now I hold no bitterness

About the black lash in a concrete wilderness

For you don't have to be wise to realise

That many minds were in a confusion

Fool by a colonise mirror of distortion

So I had to suffer much tribulation

As a leader in the heart of the black
resistance

Cause if Rasta didn't insist to resist an
expose the lie

Many more black people would a die

Now feel the music
Smell the sensie
It's quite vital to taste the ital
At this crucial Rasta carnival
For I and I rides triumphantly on the back of
a lion
I and I is on my way to Mount Zion
No more dungle down a jungle
I and I a forward up a pinnacle

THE WALTER RODNEY UPRISING

Shearer goes into UWI Kitchen
Take out Rodney while he wasn't looking
Shearer didn't like the smell of Rodney
cooking
So
Shearer sends the professor packing
So UWI student start the Rodney Uprising

Shame Shearer your name gone Abroad
Sly Shearer your name gone abroad

UWI student in Mona in Jamaica
Protest in nineteen Sixty-Eight
When Shearer couldn't wait
To
Slam the door in a Professor Rodney face
So
UWI student protest the disgrace
That
Take out Rodney while he wasn't looking
When
Shearer didn't like the smell of Rodney
cooking

Shame Shearer your name gone Abroad
Sly Shearer your name gone abroad

Hugh Shearer was like a snake in a high
grass
When
Rodney was only educating the Jamaica
underclass
Shearer was Jamaican top Brass
Who didn't like
When
Walter criticizes the Caribbean middle class
So
Walter Rodney had to pay the price
For that day Shearer wasn't nice
That day Hugh Shearer was cold like ice
For that was the time
When educating the poor was an awful crime
So
Shearer Prime Minister from Jamaica
Expel Walter Rodney back to Guyana

Shame Shearer your name gone Abroad
Sly Shearer your name gone abroad

Walter was changing mindset
Shearer says the poor wasn't ready yet
Rodney Revolution will cause too much
confusion

Just let's ensure

That the poor row their little boat without an
oar

So

Shearer slams the door

When Walter visit Canada

Shearer says look here

Tell Rodney don't you dare come back here

Jamaica was where

Hugh Shearer declares

Walter Rodney from Guyana

Persona Non Grata

RIVER HAVE TO FLOW

(For Rasta Revolution in
Jamaica)
River have to flow
yes
River have to flow
River have to flow
Yes
River have to flow

Your daughter Mary Ann
A chat to Rasta man
So you sell your black ram
An go a obeahman
But you can't stop it Mama
You can't stop it Papa
For all me know
When love is on the go
River have to flow
Yes
River have to flow
River have to flow
Yes
River have to flow
And you can't stop it Mama
You can't stop it Papa

You give Mary Ann
To rich old Sam
But what a bam bam
Ann nuh love Sam
An yuh can't stop it Mama
Yuh can't stop it Papa
For all me know
With love on the go
River have to flow
Yes
River have to flow
River have to flow
Yes
River have to flow
An yuh can't stop it mama
Yuh can't stop it papa
Me shove handcart
But right from the start
She loves me from she heart
From the day your daughter
Drink my coconut water
I didn't have to beg
I didn't have to barter
So yuh coulda huff an puff an blow
Yuh coulda huff an puff an blow
All me know with love on the go
River have to flow
Yes river have to flow

River have to flow

Yes

River have to flow

An yuh can't stop it mama

Yuh can't stop it papa

For when her skin depan fire

Is me Bongo Nyiah

Is me Bongo Nyiah out she fire

Me come to her aid

Me is her fire brigade

Me see stars

She see mars

Then we come back to earth

To pants an shirt

To blows an skirt

An yuh can't stop it mama

Yuh can't stop it mama

For all me know with love on the go

River have to flow

Yes

River have to flow

River have to flow

Yes

River have to flow

GRANNY FINGER JUST POINT AT ME

My sister was like a queen

The darling queen of my grandmother's
heart

As sure as men will die

My little sister was the angel in granny's eye

So when money start to walk in a broad-
daylight

Jusa leg it out a suitcase that lock tight

Though I beg and plea

My granny finger jus point at me

Meh say Smaddy tief granny pardner money

My sweet sister was nice like honey

My sister was prim an proper and quiet like
a mouse

An it was only me, she an granny live in a the
house

So if it wasn't she

That smaddy that thief my granny pardner
money

That tiefing smaddy had to be me

So though I beg an plea

My granny finger jus point at me

Boy jus tell me the truth

For lying is an abomination to the Lord

Well

Do you want to die and go hell?

That's all it take to lose your soul in a fire
lake

I felt as if I was one of the devil's disciples

As Granny start talk in a riddle as she tried
the Key and the Bible

But dat deh Crystal Ball was too dark

So before Cock start crow

Granny, sister and I was on the go

For though I beg an plea

Granny finger jus point at me

We tek a mini bus from Portland

We tek a bus to Kingston

We tek another bus to Clarendon

To see a Jamaican Obeah Woman

We walk under a bamboo fence

Obeah woman say come in..

An before me Granny could a utter a
sentence

De Obeah woman start to reel off the history
of we entire family story

Me was so shock

Cause me had to wonder

A how she knows that my sister boyfriend
nickname was Rat-Bat

A how she coulda tell in a live an living
colour that the big head ugly boy had my
sister under a spell

The Obeah-woman concentrate hard

An start to cut the Card

She close her eye tight like good night

Then start to ketch in a spirit deep down in
the valley of a prayer

Then Amen… it was official

This time there was no more denial

The Obeah Woman proclaimed my nice little
sister

A tief and a liar

An my heart beat a thousand Alleluia

Sweet Lord

Dem say Silent River run deep

Dem say God nah sleep

The Obeah Woman tell me Granny that me
sister tek her pardner money

Tek her pardner money an give it to her
boyfriend Rat-Bat

My Sister starts to holler an bawl as the
Obeah woman reveal all

For in the end Rat-Bat had two more
girlfriend

An Rat-Bat had a habit of taking his
girlfriend around the bend

My Granny was sad

Like she ketch a cold in her heart

She suddenly turns old

An that day amidst the pieces of broken lies

My sweet little sister had suddenly turn
human in my grandmother's eyes.

EARLY ERUPTION

Four firm thrusting thighs

Two fine bodies entwine

Just like sweet red wine

Indulging in a mind-blowing experience

This old man singing his song

Beating his gong outside his thong

Saying while praying

Keep me long

Keep me strong

I am so proud

She's so loud

Give me lightning

Give me thunder

Give me ying

Give me sweet sensual suffering

I really don't care if I am under or over

Or falling off the white cliff of Dover

I just need to go on a little bit longer

I just need to be a little bit stronger

I am aiming to please

But she is aiming to tease

But you won't need a university degree to agree with me

That only one of us can derive maximum satisfaction

From

An early volcano eruption

life is so great right now

So please dear Lord I pray

Today

Keep me high like a happy cloud

Keep me proud

Floating over land and sea

Keep me long

Keep me strong

In this sweet sensational scenario

Enjoying this young beauty down below

Hear my plea

That's the way I want to be

I wish I was a just a little bit stronger

To delay this final crescendo

That final crashing crescendo

like a falling aeroplane crash landing

I just need to go on a little bit longer

I just need to go on a little bit longer

it was much too early for sweet volcano
eruption

READING THE FINE PRINTS

It is end of term

And the summer is long and hot

And some people think you are

When you are not

She was a gold digger

Digging for gold

But I ain't got any

Not even a penny

I can feel her sharp fingernails

Digging like a spade on a grave raid

Digging beneath my skin

Buried beneath my shin

Heavy breathing against my chin

Wet

Wicked and wild like sin

And every time I feel her head on my
shoulder

My heart grew colder like a young winter
getting older

But she only grew bolder

She was a gold digger

Digging for gold

But I ain't got any

Not even a penny

I ain't got any

Not even a penny

And then one day

She Said

Your home is at risk if you don't keep up
payment on loans secure on it

And shortly after I read the fine prints

She said

Her love for me was dead

Dead

WOMAN THIRTY SOMETHING

Here is the thing
Yesterday
I met a woman thirty something
In a hurry for the ring
That will define her as wife
And change her life
This
Woman thirty something needs to be happy
Real snappy

Is not that woman thirty something is
desperate
As she expressed it
She doesn't want to be left behind
So
a husband she must find
Cause time is running out

Woman thirty Something
Is just tired a trying too much short fling
That thing without a serious commitment
Doesn't give her any fulfilment
Just more predicament
Just more maltreatment

Too much distant between her and her wedding ring

Woman thirty something

No want no more one-night stand

A man must understand

I must have a Husband

I have changed my mind

I want a kind man for my husband

I want an older mature man

A man that is financially secure

A God-Fearing man that is family oriented at his core

Woman thirty something has changed her mind

After years of tears

Meanwhile with guile she has changed the profile

Of the husband she is seeking

My husband doesn't need to be tall dark and handsome

I am now so sure

My husband doesn't have to be well hung no more

Just gentile versatile

My husband doesn't need to be young and agile no more

I am now so sure

I met a woman thirty something
In a hurry for the ring
Is not that woman thirty something is
desperate
As she expressed it
I am tired of a broken heart
I am tired of lying tongue from the start
So
Day after day woman thirty something
Searches a dating website for Mr. Right
Seeking someone who love kids
I don't want no pigs
I don't mind if he already has grandkids
I just want a nice and decent husband
Who will just love me for me
And my ready-made family

THE GREAT WHITE PHILOSOPHY

When I was young

They told I of the great white God

The great white Queen

The great white painters

The great white poets

The great white scientists

I sung the great white songs

I paid homage to the great white flag

That rule my little black island

On the back veranda of the great white
houses

I took a peep at their great white TV

And I see

The great white faces in beautiful great white
places

I heard them talk of the great white shark

I saw the great white Batman with the great
white Robin

Great white Superman

Great white Tarzan in the heart of the
African Jungle

Fighting a bungle of uncivilised man-eating
little black men

An I as a child...

I thought

It must be great to be white

But as I got older

I got wiser…

Soon I realise that all my heroes were white

Then I watch Rasta-man a fight for a positive
black identity

The fight wasn't pretty

The fight wasn't easy

After years of miseducation and mental
slavery

I went to the library to search for my history

But my history was a missing mystery

For all I see was the great white philosophy

Until I discover Marcus Garvey

See it was brother Marcus first told me

Redeem

Redeem your mind

For when the racist came

The came with the bible in is left hand

And

The Gun in the other

Listen brother

Hear me sister

This intrusion caused years of confusion

They told me to understand

That I was Satan

That slavery was my salvation

They told me be thankful to be poor

And to study war no more
They told me they were the light
So never attack nor fight back
This was only right since God was white

95

MR LIFE

(for Little Pat)

Mr. Life is a funny little man
A man I will never understand
For twenty long years
Lovingly
They live together
It seems they would be together forever
Like romance made by a magic fairytale

There was no fuss
There was no fight
Then suddenly without a warning
One bright Sunday morning
Mr. LIFE pack his suitcase and bid farewell
Leaving her
Patricia my sister who died young

FLIES FEASTING

Flies had a feast today
Yes
Flies had a feast today
In the perpetual pasture of a poor man's sore
Flies had a feast today

Flies had a feast
While he had nothing to eat

THERE ARE NO BAD DREAMS HERE

There are no bad dreams here

So I am not going to bottle up my dream like
spring water on a supermarket shelf

I am going to ask more of myself

Lest my dream shrivel an die before my eye

Like my dear departed granny gungo tree

There are no bad dreams here

In dreamland no one dreams of dying

A nightmare is merely a vision of reluctant
reality

Just a temporary aberration of the mind

A dream is different

A dream is that first brick at the start of that
a beautiful house

A dream is seeing a pretty girl and knowing
she is going to become your wife

A dream is like walking on endless miles of
white sand

With waves caressing your bare feet

A dream is like a beautiful naked nipple on a
sun-worshipper beautiful body

A naked nipple dripping with oil

A dream is like a jet-ski churning the sea

A glass bottom boat sailing over floating
fishes

Over crystal clear blue sea

Over amazing coral reefs

A dream my friend is the smell of seafood
that lifts your spirit

Seafood that tantalise your tastebuds

Seafood that nibbles at your nostrils

A dream is the sound of a live reggae band
on the beach at night

Paying homage to Marley's mystic music

A dream is the radiance of beauty

A brilliant beauty that enchants my spirit
and sings to my soul

A dream heralds hope

Without a dream there is not a hope

THE SLEEPY AFTERMATH

And the Rhythm of Love
Powerful like a ocean singing sweet songs of
freedom
And adoring angels shall tattoo your name
on my pillow
Perhaps
I shall dream that I will rise again once more
Soon
Much sooner than later
With more mountains of passion
I
Naked as Adam
You
As Eve
Like flowers in Eden singing the first songs
of spring
And whispering angels shall console me
As I sleep soundly in the stillness of the calm

My bones are too tired
Too tired to enjoy the after glow
So sleep consoles me
For I am a fountain without water
Drained by your passionate embrace
Passion is much shorter than love

Perhaps love is forever

Perhaps you are my lover forever

I shall tattoo your name on the side of a
mountain

Just above my hips

SOWETO'S BLOODBATH

(In memory of the students who die in the
Soweto Uprising June 1976)

I heard the innocent blood of black children

Crying from the ground

Reverberating

Echoing boom of distant voices

Calling their slaughters name

Soweto's mothers wept

As bullet riddled black children bodies
decorated blood-stained Soweto streets

Those days of woe

Those outrageous days in June

When I saw Soweto's student fought with
bare hands against hot lead

That struck them dead

I smelt their blood

Tasted their misery and heard their screams

Long wailing screams that curtailed their
visions and shattered their dreams

I heard a black liberation song

I saw a black burial throng

I saw Soweto's weeping mothers mourn

I saw Soweto's fathers fighting back their
tears

I saw Soweto's student black bodies buried
in the dust of defeat

But I know that their spirit lives on in victory

To strengthen the relentless struggle for
liberty

BALLAD OF A COCAINE SWALLOWER

She was Just another gig
For Mr Big
Just another gig

She was taking a short cut to suicide with her
eyes open wide
He was committing just another homicide
And enjoying the ride on the money tide
She was just another gig for Mr. Big
Just another gig

Just another ride on the money tide
She was a cocaine courier
He was the big-time trafficker
She was a first-time smuggler
Jane was the swallower whose life got
smaller and shorter

Mr. Big was her teacher
The powerful powder provider
He was her shadower who only care about
his powder
The white powder
That was goanna make him richer and richer
He was the preacher that persuade her

Convert her to faithful follower
He made get-rich quick look easier and easier
So
Jane didn't seek no shelter
Even when things got risker and risker

She was just another gig for Mr Big
Just another gig
Just another gig
Just another ride on the money tide
Taking a short cut to suicide

And I remember the day
Just two days after her nineteenth birthday
When I saw it on telly
that the cocaine package burst in her belly
Burst like a horrible hurricane in her belly

And at her funeral I saw her family feel the pain
According to the eulogy she was just another plain quiet Jane
Nothing less nothing more
Just like the girl next door
Nobody knew the smuggler
The cocaine courier
The trafficker
The cocaine swallower

Brother only knew the loving sister
Mother only knew an obedient daughter

Nobody knew she was walking on cocaine
avenue
Searching for a quick revenue

Nobody knew she was just another gig
For Mr Big
Just another gig
Just another ride on the money tide
Taking a short cut to suicide

GARRISON COMMUNITY

Time was when the politician came
And
Gave the youth man gun like toys to little
boys

Youth man then shoot dem gun for fun
And the sun shone blood in a West Kingston

Bullets and bad vibe and two political tribe
Creating disunity
To divide the urban community
Even police afraid to make raid
When gunman turn Robin hood and hand
out Kool Aid

Man in need afraid to bite the hand that feed
Now mothers a bawl
And fathers call for a final roll call
For
War pon de dutty don
The almshouse gunman
Cause a tired to make so much trip to the
cemetery
To bury people from my community
War pon de dutty don the almshouse
gunman

Rise up in a social rebellion fe improve we
social condition

War pon de dutty don the almshouse
gunman

Unite against this evil oppression in this
Garrison Community

Rise up against the repressive regime dat a
kill the cream

An a strangle we dream

Dat a mash up we life

Dat a push us in a endless strife

W

War pon de dutty don the almshouse gun
man

Rise up against this violent muderation and
constant boderation

Rise up against the gun shot wound death
and gansta destruction

Rise up

Before dem pronounce you child dead on
arrival at the hospital

Shot by an evil gun criminal

Stop de denial

It's time we put gangster on trial

Nuh shelter no dam criminal

Stop creating your own prison in a Garrison
Community

VICTIM

Victim, Victim
Victim to the rhythm of the system
Victim, Victim
Victim to the rhythm of the system
Blam
Blam
Blam
A youth man drop
Shot by a cop
'im shirt turn red
An blood jusa leak outa im head
Look deh
Watch deh
Dem a frame 'im
Dem a put a gun ina 'im han'
Fe say im a bad man
One more youth man gone
One more innocent youth man dead
He was victim
A victim
A victim to the rhythm of the system
A victim to the rhythm of the system

I see three Jon Crows
Perching on a coconut tree

Spreading their wings and sharpening their
beaks

Jus waiting for an evening meal
Jus waiting for an evening meal
An then a hear me mama a holler
An then a hear me papa a bawl
That dem find me breda
Dem find 'im dead
Dem find 'im full up with bullet lead
With 'im mouth gag
Tie up ina wan crocus bag
For he was a victim
A victim
A victim to the rhythm of the system
A victim to the rhythm of the system

CEMETERY TOWN

(To Covid 19 victims)

Still at the top of the hill

About to go down to Cemetery Town

I soon realise that my world is unprepared

A mighty World now colonises by a
schizophrenic pandemic

Academic divisible

Virus transferable

Cure inadmissible like great words without
syllables

Little me

I have got the church key in my pocket

Only a solitary tear left in my eye socket

So

dude

Would it be awfully rude

That I decline you injecting death on me like
a killer Bee

Would it be awfully crude

If I dare to decline

Because of this awful fear that boils in my
mind

You see
I have come this way before
I have been coming here more and more

So many still
Too young to make a will
Didn't make it to the top of the hill

So
Dude
Would it be awfully rude
If I decline this time to go down
To Cemetery Town

MONGOOSE RAPTURE

Dive down deep
Dive and take a peep
Dive down deep
Dive and take a peep
Wake from your slumber
Wake from your sleep
Dive down deep
Dive and take peep

Let's go deeper than skin deep
Where
Black and white turns red in perfect
harmony
Beneath the skin the human story is in
perfect unity

My story is deeper than my skin
So never ever just look at the cover of my
book
And confine your mind to the prison in the
colour of my skin
Dive down deep
Dive and take a peep
Dive down deep
Dive and take a peep
Wake from your slumber
Wake from your sleep
Dive down deep

Dive and take a peep
Only when you go deeper than the confusion
That you can become a part of the solution
If you know the truth
Then you will know that only the tree of love
bears good fruit

For if you feed your unborn babies with lies
Don't be surprised
If they are born with murder in their eyes
If you are wise
You will soon realise
That your freedom is my freedom
And your war is my war
If you are wise
You will soon realise
That if you let me mingle too long in your
garbage
I will soon create my own heavy baggage
Your depravity creates a food mountain that
you destroy with fire
My hungry depravity creates an angry desire
in me to be less than human

Dive down deep
Dive and take a peep
Dive down deep
Dive and take a peep
Wake from your slumber

Wake from your sleep
Dive down deep
Dive and take a peep

While you are eating your apples of dirty
deception
I am eating my maggot- infested mangoes of
misconception
So
I am not always going to keep the faith
When my belly is empty
It is not easy to watch my children die
In a world of plenty

Excuse me if I believe
That everything I see in your eyes are lies
Excuse me if I no longer believe
That ugly caterpillars can become beautiful
butterflies

If you can't even admit
That exploitation of the poor exists
That black African slavery was a crime
against humanity
What hope have we got to live in unity

Dive down deep
Dive and take a peep
Dive down deep

Dive and take a peep
Wake from your slumber
Wake from your sleep
Dive down deep
Dive and take a peep

It is very hard for me to let you in
Cause I am paranoid
That your lovely food basket is still laden
with sin
Cause
I know so well that the smile you wear is
plastic
Like a poison cup of justice
You are still the mongoose man
You come to capture like mongoose rapture
And
I am still the chicken that fight all night